LITERATURE
ACTIVITIES
Teens Actually
L♥VE

Authentic Projects for the Language Arts Classroom

LITERATURE ACTIVITIES

Teens Actually LVE

Beth Ahlgrim, Bill Fritz,
Jeremy Gertzfield, and Lisa Lukens

PRUFROCK PRESS INC.
WACO, TEXAS

Library of Congress catalog information
currently on file with the publisher.

Copyright © 2014, Prufrock Press Inc.

Edited by Bethany Johnsen

Cover and layout design by Raquel Trevino

ISBN-13: 978-1-61821-168-2

Printed in the United States of America.

At the time of this book's publication, all facts and figures cited are the most current available. All telephone numbers, addresses, and website URLs are accurate and active. All publications, organizations, websites, and other resources exist as described in the book, and all have been verified. The authors and Prufrock Press Inc. make no warranty or guarantee concerning the information and materials given out by organizations or content found at websites, and we are not responsible for any changes that occur after this book's publication. If you find an error, please contact Prufrock Press Inc.

Prufrock Press Inc.
P.O. Box 8813
Waco, TX 76714-8813
Phone: (800) 998-2208
Fax: (800) 240-0333
http://www.prufrock.com

TABLE OF CONTENTS

INTRODUCTION

In today's ever-changing landscape of technology, in which social networking sites, visual media, and video games all vie for our students' time and attention, literature is rapidly losing ground against the myriad entertainment choices students now have at their disposal. Now more than ever, we have to ask ourselves how we, as educators, can compete for our students' attention without losing our core values and high standards. This book will challenge the notion that the only way we can create resilient and creative thinkers of today is through the time-honored practices of the past. By looking at how students use media, we have created new ways to interact with classic and modern texts, beyond the quiz and the expository essay.

If students aren't permitted to engage with literature in ways that are socially and culturally relevant, can literature fully meet the educational needs of our 21st-century students? Instead of asking classic literature to meet the unique recreational, cultural, and of course, educational needs of today's youth, this book offers activities that will empower students to work with literature on their own terms in order to rediscover the joys it holds. Through a variety of innovative and highly engaging projects, *Literature Activities Teens Actually Love* develops a new lens through which to view literary activities. Students will see that engaging with literature can be highly entertaining even as it cultivates their higher order thinking skills.

This book will guide instructors through various lesson plans that show how teachers and students can bridge the technology gap by finding creative solutions to traditional academic problems. In using their technological skills to move from print to nonprint assessments, students will have the opportunity to explore texts with greater comfort, familiarity, and ownership, blossoming into autonomous learners in the process.

Although each of the activities in this book uses a particular work of literature as its assigned text, it is important to remember that the general principles of each activity can be easily adapted to any work of your choosing. So, although the activities in Chapter 1, for example, were created with *Fahrenheit 451* (Bradbury, 1953/2012) in mind, they can be used just as effectively to assess any other book you currently teach or desire to teach, with only minimal adjustments. If you wish to use *Fahrenheit 451* (Bradbury, 1953/2012), saving yourself time, the activities are ready to go. Consult the appendix on page 75 for a list of suggested texts that pair well with each activity.

Chapter 1

UNDERSTANDING

In this chapter, the activities—which can be used as common formative assessments and completed either independently or collaboratively, on a student's first or second reading—gauge how well the students comprehend the text from a literal and inferential level. These assessments also gauge whether students can grasp emerging relationships within the texts. Furthermore, the activities work as a guide for students as they begin to identify higher order relationships within either an author's work, such as a novel or short story, or a student's work, most typically an essay or speech. Because the activities in this chapter are highly visual, teachers can measure a student's ability to create concrete analogies grounded in the text. The goal is to determine students' readiness for deeper analysis.

Although *Fahrenheit 451* (Bradbury, 1953/2012) serves as the sample text for both activities in this chapter, they can easily be adapted to any reading assignment that you wish.

FRIENDING FACEBOOK IN THE CLASSROOM

Facebook in the classroom? Aren't we trying to discourage our students from using electronic devices during class? But, as the old adage goes, "If you can't beat 'em, join 'em." By bringing Facebook into the classroom, we are meeting students at their level to bring them to ours. We are also using an accessible site to assess our students' abilities to comprehend what they read, as well as determine how well they can make inferences from the text, both literary and informational.

Sara Schmelling (2009) has created models that your students can imitate in her book *Ophelia Joined the Group, Maidens Who Don't Float*, in which she created Facebook pages for famous literary characters such as Elizabeth Bennett from *Pride and Prejudice* and Pip from *Great Expectations*.

CCSS Alignment

This assessment aligns with the Common Core State Standards (CCSS) in Reading for both literary and informational texts.

- CCSS.ELA-Literacy.RL.1 Cite strong and thorough textual evidence to support analysis of what the text says explicitly as well as inferences drawn from the text, including determining where the text leaves matters uncertain.
- CCSS.ELA-Literacy.RL.2 Determine two or more themes or central ideas of a text and analyze their development over the course of the text, including how they interact and build on one another to produce a complex account; provide an objective summary of the text.
- CCSS.ELA-Literacy.RL.3 Analyze the impact of the author's choices regarding how to develop and relate elements of a story or drama (e.g., where a story is set, how the action is ordered, how the characters are introduced and developed).
- CCSS.ELA-Literacy.RI.3 Analyze a complex set of ideas or sequence of events and explain how specific individuals, ideas, or events interact and develop over the course of the text.

The Facebook page discussion in this activity also weaves in the Speaking and Listening CCSS:

- CCSS.ELA-Literacy.SL1b Work with peers to promote civil, democratic discussions and decision-making, set clear goals and deadlines, and establish individual roles as needed.
- CCSS.ELA-Literacy.SL.1c Propel conversations by posing and responding to questions that probe reasoning and evidence; ensure a hearing for a full range of positions on a topic or issue; clarify, verify, or challenge ideas and conclusions; and promote divergent and creative perspectives.
- CCSS.ELA-Literacy.SL.1d Respond thoughtfully to diverse perspectives; synthesize comments, claims, and evidence made on all sides of an issue; resolve contradictions when possible; and determine what additional information or research is required to deepen the investigation or complete the task.
- CCSS.ELA-Literacy.SL5 Make strategic use of digital media (e.g., textual, graphical, audio, visual, and interactive elements) in presentations to enhance understanding of findings, reasoning, and evidence and to add interest.

Materials Needed

- Student copies of *Fahrenheit 451* (or alternate assigned text)
- Handout 1.1a: Facebook Assignment
- Handout 1.1b: Facebook Template or access to Facebook

The Process

Students can complete the activity in either of two ways. They can create an actual Facebook page at http://www.facebook.com, or use the template provided in Handout 1.1b: Facebook Template. This latter method helps to navigate around the barrier of Facebook being blocked on the school server.

Regardless of which method you choose, have students first create a "home page" for their assigned or chosen character. On their home page they can add the character's birthday and interests and upload pictures.

Once you grade the home page, students can begin posting, either on the online page they created or continuing to use a template. Through their posts, students should have "conversations" with other characters from the novel. At this point, require students to integrate textual evidence. Not only are you assessing their comprehension and inferencing of the text, but you are also formatively assessing students' abilities to choose appropriate and effective quotations and properly integrate their evidence.

So, let's bring *Fahrenheit 451* (Bradbury, 1953/2012) into the 21st century and see what it would look like if the characters created Facebook pages and talked to each other. Would Facebook bring them closer together or farther apart? Present a copy of Handout 1.1a: Facebook Assignment to each of your students.

The sample student Facebook page (see Figure 1) created for Guy Montag clearly shows the student's comprehension of who the character is, as well as how he relates to other characters. The symbols for the characters also show the student moving toward creating analogies or metaphorical representations of the characters in the novel.

The character Facebook page serves as a formative assessment for the summative assessment. You can provide timely feedback for students in order to move them toward mastery. As you probably know, many of the CCSS integrate reading and writing. The Facebook page helps students integrate the writing and reading skills while avoiding being overwhelmed by a long literary analysis assignment. The quick feedback you can provide on the frequent postings will help you see where your students require extra support and areas where they need reteaching. From this, you gain the knowledge required to differentiate your classroom activities.

If you have a small group of students who have yet to master the basic comprehension, you can create a group class period activity. To differentiate, have students who are unable to grasp the basic comprehension reread the text together and record what they notice about the character, the setting, and the conflict. Also direct them to stop at a certain passage to make predictions that are based on what they have read. With the differentiated groups, you know that although all students are completing the Facebook assessment, some may have a deeper analysis of character. This deeper analysis would appear on the Facebook feed as a conversation between two characters or as a status update. If you have a group that is ready to move to analysis of character, they continue to move toward complex thinking. With the Facebook assessment you can easily incorporate the theory of Vygotsky's zone of proximal development prior to the summative assessment.

If your school server permits students to log into Facebook at school, you can have students "friend" each other's characters and use the Facebook site

Figure 1. Sample student Facebook page for Fahrenheit 451 character.

live. You too can friend the characters and read the online discussion that the students are having as they post as their character. Not only does this show that students understand the character, but it also shows their ability to use the implications from the text to enter into a conversation.

As students converse with each other via their characters' Facebook pages, they are required to integrate textual evidence on the Facebook feed to support their posts. This helps students focus on the importance of selecting the most relevant and effective evidence. Often students will choose a quotation simply because they were instructed to do so, but they may not look at all the complexities of choosing salient and purposeful passages. The repeated practice of selecting effective evidence for many short and frequently assessed posts will enable them to hone this skill.

The Facebook page assessment could also be adapted for informational text. As you move toward increasing literacy for all curricular areas, you can share this assignment with other disciplines. When creating a Facebook page for informational text, you may not have characters to analyze. Students may create a Facebook page to shed light on the essay's or article's claim. For example, when examining the role that race plays in American society, you could ask your students to read Hua Hsu's article, "The End of White America?" (Hsu, 2009). This piece is an excellent companion for a study of *The Great Gatsby* (Fitzgerald, 1925/2004).

While analyzing Hsu's article, students work to identify her claim, the strengths of her argument, and the limitations. They can then create a Facebook page that reveals the complexities of race in America. Students state Hsu's claim and ask classmates to comment, beginning with whether they agree or disagree. At this point, it is imperative that students stay grounded in the text as the Common Core indicates. Avoid student reader responses. You could ask students to respond to the page as a character from the novel may respond to the article. Students take on the persona of one of the major or minor characters in *The Great Gatsby* and use textual evidence to support their character's response.

The pairing of texts is the beginning of asking to students to synthesize evidence. Once you know that they can analyze, you want them to show how the texts essentially "talk to each other." This critical thinking is the practice your students need to prepare them for life beyond high school. It also provides a platform for students to discuss particular issues, some controversial, in an appropriate objective tone.

The use of the social networking site can help your students keep up with all of the reading they complete throughout the year, along with all of the analyses they complete. Facebook creates an organized space for critical thinking, a space that students may need to revisit in order to prepare for a summative assignment.

FACEBOOK ASSIGNMENT

In this activity, you will create a Facebook page for your assigned character and conduct conversations as your character with the other characters from the novel. Include the following:

- at least two status updates from your character
- at least two series of pictures posted by your character
- at least six "friends" who post to your character's wall
- at least six properly integrated textual supports for each post
- at least two exchanges per act

Be neat! Your information should reflect an understanding of your character and his or her interactions with other characters.

FACEBOOK TEMPLATE

facebook

Home   Profile   Friends   Inbox   (Your Character's Name)   Settings   Search

Insert picture of present-day actor here that would properly portray your character, based on what you know about him - (obviously, delete these words when you find the picture).

Your Character's Name

What's on your mind?

Share

Recent Activity

Information

Relationship Status:

Birthday:

Activity 1.2:

VISUALIZING TEXT

Long before students walked hallways with earbuds plugged into MP3 players, families gathered around television screens to watch large men pummel each other for a football championship, and newspapers folded due to lack of readership, Ray Bradbury wrote of a society that was so enamored of its technology that it lost its humanity. Although *Fahrenheit 451* was released as science fiction, it bears an uncanny resemblance to 21st-century society.

The following activity allows students to demonstrate their engagement with a novel in multiple ways: First they write a traditional essay, then communicate their argument to the class in a presentation that combines the oral and the visual. Early in their reading, students are asked the following: In a nation defined by video games, reality TV, virtual friendships, and technology that allows us constant contact and entertainment, to what extent are we in danger of becoming the society that Bradbury warns of in his novel? Initially, students may see little connection, but as they progress in their reading and with activities that include research and supplemental texts, students begin formulating answers to the question. By the end of the novel, students have a number of ideas, as well as evidence to support their position.

Bradbury takes care to highlight Mildred Montag as an exemplary citizen: The three parlor walls are always on and she refers to the characters in her "reality" programs as aunts, uncles, cousins, nephews, and nieces. Because the average citizen is visual, it makes sense to ask students to visualize their argument. After all, this generation is tech savvy and can easily transfer its knowledge into visual representations that meet Common Core State Standards for Speaking and Listening. As a bonus, the students have already fulfilled the CCSS for reading and writing through the essay component of the project.

When being introduced to a text, it is helpful for students to engage in a prereading activity. Thus, we create a Wordle™ document from a shorter nonfiction piece. Wordle.net is a website that allows users to convert a substantial piece of text into a visual "word cloud" that emphasizes the most frequently used words in the original text. Anyone can quickly create a Wordle™ at http://www.wordle.net by following the website's simple instructions. Once students have become familiar with word clouds through the

VISUALIZING TEXT

UNDERSTANDING   **9**

prereading activity, they are ready to turn their *Fahrenheit 451* essays into word clouds for use in their presentation.

Visual representations of text are extremely helpful teaching tools. The first literature most children are exposed to is picture books. The big, colorful images capture a child's attention and teach him or her to put a story together. Even as children begin recognizing letters and deciphering words, the story's pictures fill in gaps to develop understanding and create connections to the story's sequence of events. Eventually, children graduate to chapter books that have fewer pictures and more difficult text.

Although "visual literacy" has been in the English lexicon for some time, the concept has gained significance in the last decade. Technology offers opportunities for teachers to engage students differently than in years past, when visual literacy meant writing an essay comparing and contrasting a piece of literature to the text's movie version. Although writing is still necessary for assessing whether a student is capable of producing a coherent and insightful connection to the literature, technology offers a means of introducing, reinforcing, and synthesizing the literary text. Moreover, technology offers ways for differentiating instruction and allows teachers to navigate a classroom landscape of students who are increasingly more visual because their television viewing, social media, and textbooks often reduce deep ideas to visual components. Thus, with teachers competing with elements outside their control, it is necessary to develop methods for engaging students in the text as well as giving them focus for their own writing. Something as simple as creating a word cloud allows students to take a more complex text and home in on prominent ideas.

CCSS Alignment

Analyzing a Wordle™ document is a simple but effective way to engage students in the prereading process and aligns with the following standards:

- CCSS.ELA-Literacy.RI.9-10.2: Determine a central idea of a text and analyze its development over the course of the text, including how it emerges and is shaped and refined by specific details; provide an objective summary of the text.
- CCSS.ELA-Literacy.RI.9-10.4: Determine the meaning of words and phrases as they are used in a text, including figurative, connotative, and technical meanings; analyze the cumulative impact of specific word choices on meaning and tone (e.g., how the language of a court opinion differs from that of a newspaper).

- CCSS.ELA-Literacy.RI.9-10.5: Analyze in detail how an author's ideas or claims are developed and refined by particular sentences, paragraphs, or larger portions of a text (e.g., a section or chapter).
- CCSS.ELA-Literacy.RI.9-10.6: Determine an author's point of view or purpose in a text and analyze how an author uses rhetoric to advance that point of view or purpose.
- CCSS.ELA-Literacy.RI.9-10.8: Delineate and evaluate the argument and specific claims in a text, assessing whether the reasoning is valid and the evidence is relevant and sufficient; identify false statements and fallacious reasoning.

The essay and visual presentation components of the project address the following elements of the CCSS for grades 9–10:
- CCSS.ELA-Literacy.W.9-10.1a: Introduce precise claim(s), distinguish the claim(s) from alternate or opposing claims, and create an organization that establishes clear relationships among claim(s), counterclaims, reasons, and evidence.
- CCSS.ELA-Literacy.W.9-10.1c: Use words, phrases, and clauses to link the major sections of the text, create cohesion, and clarify the relationships between claim(s) and reasons, between reasons and evidence, and between claim(s) and counterclaims.
- CCSS.ELA-Literacy.W.9-10.1d: Establish and maintain a formal style and objective tone while attending to the norms and conventions of the discipline in which they are writing.
- CCSS.ELA-Literacy.W.9-10.1e: Provide a concluding statement or section that follows from and supports the argument presented.
- CCSS.ELA-Literacy.SL.9-10.4: Present information, findings, and supporting evidence clearly, concisely, and logically such that listeners can follow the line of reasoning and the organization, development, substance, and style are appropriate to purpose and task.
- CCSS.ELA-Literacy.SL.9-10.5: Make strategic use of digital media (e.g., textual, graphical, audio, visual, and interactive elements) in presentations to enhance understanding of findings, reasoning, and evidence and to add interest.

Materials Needed

- Word cloud of prereading (e.g., Nuremberg Trials testimony) assignment
- Student copies of *Fahrenheit 451* (or alternate assigned text)
- Handout 1.2a: From Essay to Speech
- Handout 1.2b: Brainstorming Sheet
- Computer access
- PowerPoint, Keynote, or iMovie, iPhoto, or Comic Life software

The Process

Prereading. It is helpful to warm students up to this activity by having them read a shorter nonfiction work on similar themes. During a nonfiction unit on civil disobedience, students can be introduced to the concept of civil disobedience with criteria and scenarios. After spending several days reading and discussing Henry David Thoreau's (1849/2009) "On Civil Disobedience" and Stanley Milgram's (1974) psychological experiment on obedience, give students a copy of a word cloud created from an excerpt of Rudolf Hoess's testimony at the 1946 Nuremberg Trials (see Figure 2). Without offering them any background information about Hoess or the Nuremberg Trials, allow students to study the document for several minutes. The class then engages in a discussion about the dominant words. Students notice "detachment," "Reichsfuhrer," "special," "duty," "SS," "parents," "Auschwitz," and, to a lesser extent, "man," "nothing," and "shooting." As the discussion progresses, it segues into the structure of the words. Why are some words larger and more prominent? What might the smaller words indicate? What words conjure the most powerful images? What might this document be about? Even less engaged students have ideas about words and images; thus, everyone has a focus for reading.

Once students have engaged in the prereading activity and finished reading *Fahrenheit 451*, they are ready for the main project, which moves from a traditional essay to a visualization of their argument. Pass out Handout 1.2a: From Essay to Speech, going over it in class to make sure students understand what is expected. Once everyone is on the same page, distribute Handout 1.2b: Brainstorming Sheet so students can begin formulating the arguments that they will research for their essay. Because Bradbury's novel remains germane, there are myriad topics that are relevant to today's stu-

Figure 2. Word cloud of Rudolf Hoess's testimony at Nuremberg Trials.

dents. The topics provide variety and allow students freedom to create their argument.

After students have composed an essay comparing the society in Bradbury's novel to our own, direct them to turn it into a speech. Because speeches tend to run too long or too short, students first make their essay's text into a word cloud (see Figure 3). The word cloud serves two purposes. First, students can determine whether the dominant ideas highlighted by the Wordle™ program are, indeed, the ideas that the student intended to focus on. Secondly, the word cloud condenses students' ideas into a one-page document, which they can then use to write a speech and create accompanying visual elements. Make it clear to students that the word cloud (along with the presentation shown to the whole class) is the only note that they can use when delivering their speech. This may overwhelm them at first, but once students realize that they are already quite familiar with their material, they embrace the challenge of giving a speech without depending upon note cards.

The process of streamlining the original *Fahrehneit 451* essays into speeches and creating the accompanying visual presentations takes four to five class periods. To initiate the process, I assign partners to each student. Each partner comes to the relationship with a copy of his or her original essay and its word cloud. Together the students collaborate on how to structure each other's speeches and how to use the word cloud as a speech prompt. Along with creating a collegial environment, brainstorming about how to create a speech from a word cloud serves as a valuable editing strategy. Once the seminal ideas have been established, students begin putting together

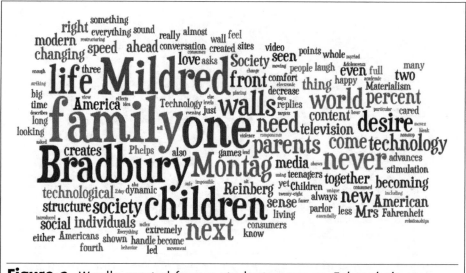

Figure 3. Wordle created from a student essay on *Fahrenheit 451*.

their visual presentation. (See Figures 4–11 for examples of student visual products.) Similar to the writing process, the class discusses ways students can visually present their argument and how to smoothly transition from one piece of evidence to another. Finally, just as students are expected to edit and refine their writing, the same process applies to their presentation.

Before making their presentations to the class, students practice with each other and offer feedback to one another. Presentations are between 4 and 5 minutes, and the time constraint is strict because it forces students to make deliberate choices. Students are assessed both verbally and visually, and the overall assessment is split between the verbal presentation and the visual document.

Although speaking is an essential skill, students often struggle to clearly express themselves. By visualizing a text, they become more adept at expressing their ideas in a formal presentation.

Figure 4. Sample student slide from *Fahrenheit 451* presentation.

Figure 5. Sample student slide from *Fahrenheit 451* presentation.

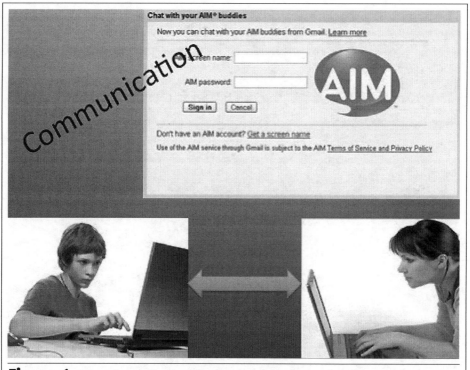

Figure 6. Sample student slide from *Fahrenheit 451* presentation.

Figure 7. Sample student slide from *Fahrenheit 451* presentation.

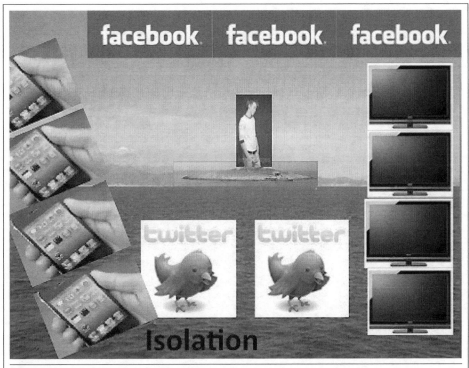

Figure 8. Sample student slide from *Fahrenheit 451* presentation.

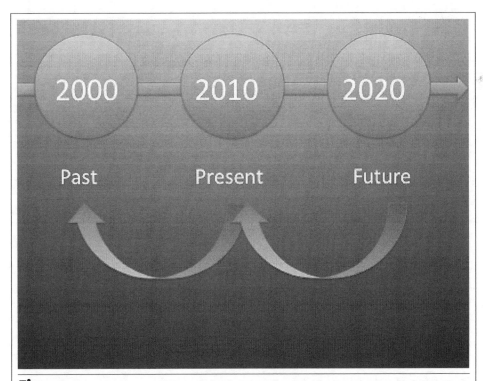

Figure 9. Sample student slide from *Fahrenheit 451* presentation.

Figure 10. Sample student slide from *Fahrenheit 451* presentation.

Figure 11. Sample student slide from *Fahrenheit 451* presentation.

Handout 1.2a

FROM ESSAY TO SPEECH

As a final project for *Fahrenheit 451*, you will demonstrate understanding of the novel and its key concepts by synthesizing the main ideas and making connections between the literature and today's society.

Activities:

1. Brainstorm connections between the society depicted in Bradbury's novel and our own society. Conduct research to support your position.

2. Incorporate your research into an essay that synthesizes the information and makes viable connections that demonstrate critical thinking and analysis. Your essay will integrate multiple sources (two pieces of evidence from the novel and three from other sources) and include a works cited page according to MLA standards.

3. Paste your essay text into the text box at http://www.wordle.net to create a word cloud that clearly displays your most prominent ideas.

4. Using your word cloud for assistance, condense your essay into a 4–5 minute speech.

5. Using PowerPoint, Keynote, iPhoto, Comic Life, or another program, make a visual presentation to accompany your speech, being sure to incorporate 10 visual elements supporting your essay's position.

6. Deliver your speech to the class, using only your word cloud as a prompt, and presenting a visual show that makes clear and compelling connections between the novel and present-day society.

Handout 1.2b

BRAINSTORMING SHEET

Prompt: In a nation defined by video games, reality TV, virtual friendships, fake news shows, and technology that fosters constant contact and entertainment, American society has become the society that Bradbury warned about in *Fahrenheit 451*.

Using two pieces of evidence from the novel and three pieces of evidence from the news, current events, biographies, or history texts, write a thoughtful essay that defends, challenges, or qualifies the above assertion. The essay should be 3–4 pages long.

You are expected to spend time in the library, finding research to support your position. You will print or copy your research, annotate it, and incorporate it into your essay. Later, you will turn this essay into a visual presentation and use the elements of logical argumentation and persuasion to present your position.

Brainstorming:

My position (circle one):   Defend   Challenge   Qualify

Connections to *Fahrenheit 451*:

Violence

Education (film teachers)

The breakdown of the nuclear family

War or the threat of war

Seashells

Entertainment/Media

Constant movement and/or speed

Mass and size (e.g., billboards, parlor walls)

Increase in suicides

Bullying

Unhappiness and sleeping pills (think Mildred; think nine to 10 suicide attempts per night)

Religion

Politics/Elections

Censorship

Nature

Equality

Government intrusion/intervention

Handout 1.2b: Brainstorming Sheet, continued

My ideas:

_____

_____

_____

_____

_____

_____

_____

_____

_____

_____

_____

_____

_____

_____

_____

_____

_____

_____

_____

_____

Chapter 2

ADAPTATION

The activities in this chapter help transition students from surface reading to a more comprehensive analysis of the ideas and structure that an author presents in a text. Because the assessments are highly visual, students begin to experiment with the critical thinking necessary to engage in analysis and even synthesis of ideas contained within the text. When students make certain choices as they transfer from print to nonprint representation of the textual ideas, they demonstrate the genesis of their analyses. This helps teachers assess students' readiness for analysis and evaluation of the author's choice of diction, syntax, and structure. If students can show their ability to transfer print text to nonprint text, they demonstrate analytical reading. Student who demonstrate this deeper analysis are now ready to create an independent student-driven analysis.

As with all of the activities in this book, the activities from this chapter can be adapted for a number of texts. Activity 2.1: Graphic Novel is especially effective for books that feature an unreliable or confusing narrator, such as *The Catcher in the Rye* (Salinger, 1951/1991). The suggested text for Activity 2.2: Quilt as High Art is *Their Eyes Were Watching God* (Hurston, 1937/2006), with the essay "In Search of Our Mothers' Gardens" (Walker, 1974/2002) as a suggested companion piece, but another piece that explores the value of "low art" and the everyday experiences of marginalized people would work as well. Activity 2.3: Movie Trailer can be used with virtually any text, but Activity 2.4: Allegory is designed for use with allegories, such as Plato's "Allegory of the Cave" (360 B.C.E.).

GRAPHIC NOVEL

When we ask our students to analyze a piece of literature in class discussion or in writing, we generally assume that they can see the big picture and find relevant information from the text to support their position. We hope they can navigate abstract concepts with ease as they sort through the text, looking for key passages that can be used to create a well-defined claim with evidence. As educators, we trust that students understand what the big picture looks like and what the elements of that picture are, and that the learners can put it all together in a logical and linear way.

But for many students, sorting through myriad (and sometimes unconnected) events of a literary work is overwhelming. Asking them to recall hours of class discussions, running through class notes and annotations, all while looking for evidence to support an abstract concept, is like asking them to both create and solve a complex math problem. It is little wonder that students can struggle in finding pertinent information or arranging it in a way that creates a cohesive and coherent essay. The characters, theme, and storyline swirl together in the minds of students who are growing increasingly frustrated with the daunting task before them.

Having students create the panels for a graphic reading of a novel allows them the freedom to explore rich and abstract thematic levels within the framework of the visual and concrete. The learner has the ability to emphasize certain aspects of the novel in his or her artwork and to shrink or delete others. This means that as they create the panels, students can engage with the text in a way that is both deliberate and liberating. The student artists are making unconscious (and thus unthreatening) literary connections and judgments while organizing their panels in ways that often mirror the text but are not bound by the original ordering of the story. While the visual learners are creating the artwork for the panels, they are making decisions that go beyond the literal reading, and must account for rhetorical layers of the text that might have gone unexplored and misunderstood in the original reading. When drawing faces, for example, relevant information is literally drawn out. Concepts as challenging as tone are discovered as the artist accounts for facial expression and the placement of characters in the panels. The relationships of characters to each other and to their environment become apparent in the artistic choices that the student makes. Most importantly, the learner has to consistently confront theme as he or she chooses what information to place in the panels, how to deliver that information, and the order of the panels.

CSSS Alignment

Because this activity can be implemented at a number of grade levels, the CCSS addressed are in the K–12 levels.

- CCSS.K-12.SL.2 Comprehension and Collaboration: Integrate and evaluate information presented in diverse media and formats, including visually, quantitatively, and orally.
- CCSS.K-12.SL.3 Comprehension and Collaboration: Evaluate a speaker's point of view, reasoning, and use of evidence and rhetoric.
- CCSS.K-12 R.2 Key Ideas and Details: Determine central ideas or themes of a text and analyze their development; summarize the key supporting details and ideas.
- CCSS.K-12.R.R.3 Key Ideas and Details: Analyze how and why individuals, events, and ideas develop and interact over the course of a text.
- CCSS.K-12.R.R.4 Craft and Structure: Interpret words and phrases as they are used in a text, including determining technical, connotative, and figurative meanings, and analyze how specific word choices shape meaning or tone.
- CCSS.K-12.R.R.5 Craft and Structure: Analyze the structure of texts, including how specific sentences, paragraphs, and larger portions of the text (e.g., a section, chapter, scene, or stanza) relate to each other and the whole.
- CCSS.K-12.R.R.6 Craft and Structure: Assess how point of view or purpose shapes the content and style of a text.
- CCSS.K-12.R.R.7 Integration of Knowledge and Ideas: Integrate and evaluate content presented in diverse formats and media, including visually and quantitatively, as well as in words.

Materials Needed

- Assigned text
- Paper (e.g., standard computer paper, colored construction paper, or whatever the student prefers)

ADAPTATION   **25**

- Painting or drawing instruments, or any available computer software (e.g., InDesign, Photoshop)

The Process

The actual assignment is straightforward—ask your students to create graphic panels based on an assigned text, or one particularly challenging section or chapter of an assigned text. The exercise is particularly helpful when students need to make broad thematic connections. Avoid giving overly specific instructions on the number of panels or length of the graphic work; the idea is to give students the creative freedom to explore their own interpretations of the text.

Generally students should create their own artwork, but if they are particularly artistically challenged, they can create panels by taking images off the Internet, or using available software appropriate for the assignment. The drawing quality is, of course, not what is being graded here. But the more that is in the students' control, the better, as the students' understandings of what they are doing shouldn't be dictated by the constraints of images they've picked, nor by their inability to draw out what they wish to. The students should be given free reign as to how they organize the panels, as the organization will represent sophisticated thematic connections. The students' creativity should guide them.

There are several effective hybrids of the assignment. Students can create a graphic reading from a differing point of view than the one presented in the original text. This rendition of the assignment is helpful for getting students to understand concepts such as narrator reliability. The device is great to use with a book like *The Catcher In The Rye* (Salinger, 1951/1991), as students often struggle with Holden's perception of the world around him. The assignment can also flesh out the role of secondary characters in the plot. For the scene in *Jane Eyre* (Brontë, 1847/2000) in which Jane and Adele are invited to join Rochester's guests, students can be asked to create a visual comparison between what Adele would have witnessed and what Jane saw. The act of drawing will reveal hidden prejudices, alliances, and manipulative behaviors that are barely suggested in the original reading, and will be the springboard for rich class discussions.

QUILT AS HIGH ART

One of Zora Neale Hurston's objectives in both her fiction and nonfiction writing was to elevate the everyday into viable, respected art. She went against many of the intellectual leaders of the Harlem Renaissance, who criticized her use of Black English Vernacular, saying that by presenting her characters as normal, working-class people, Hurston tarnished the image of the African American intellectual who was "above" such commonness. But Hurston stood by her assertion of the beauty and artistry of the everyday, and it is this commitment to preserving the lives of ordinary people that makes much of her work continue to be so powerful.

To assess students' understanding of *Their Eyes Were Watching God* (Hurston, 1937/1996), asking them to write a traditional essay seems incongruous. Why should we examine a text that challenges traditional views of cultural expression with one of the most standard forms of academic discourse? There needs to be another way to honor the spirit of Hurston's work while assessing student understanding.

This lesson incorporates the study of a nonfiction essay, Alice Walker's "In Search of Our Mother's Gardens" (1974/2002), with the identification of key scenes, passages, and images from *Their Eyes Were Watching God*. Students create, as a classroom community, a work of art that displays their analytical abilities.

Throughout the course of this project, students gain an understanding of Alice Walker's definition of art, one that is much more inclusive than traditional definitions that describe only "high art." They learn about the art of American quilt making, create quilt squares that represent key moments from *Their Eyes Were Watching God*, and, ultimately, assemble a class quilt that tells the novel's story.

CCSS Alignment

This project addresses the following CCSS. Because *Their Eyes Were Watching God* is typically an 11th-grade text, the standards listed are those for grades 11 and 12.

- CCSS.11-12.R.I.1 Key Ideas and Details: Cite strong and thorough textual evidence to support analysis of what the text says explicitly as well as inferences drawn from the text, including determining where the text leaves matters uncertain.

- CCSS.11-12.R.I.10 Range of Reading and Level of Text Complexity: By the end of grade 11, read and comprehend literary nonfiction in the grades 11–12 CCR text complexity band proficiently, with scaffolding as needed at the high end of the range. By the end of grade 12, read and comprehend literary nonfiction at the high end of the grades 11–12 CCR text complexity band independently and proficiently.
- CCSS.11-12.W.2.b Text Types and Purposes: Develop the topic thoroughly by selecting the most significant and relevant facts, extended definitions, concrete details, quotations, or other information and examples appropriate to the audience's knowledge of the topic.
- CCSS.11-12.SL.1 Comprehension and Collaboration: Initiate and participate effectively in a range of collaborative discussions (one-on-one, in groups, and teacher-led) with diverse partners on grades 11–12 topics, texts, and issues, building on others' ideas and expressing their own clearly and persuasively.
- CCSS.11-12.L.4 Vocabulary Acquisition and Use: Determine or clarify the meaning of unknown and multiple-meaning words and phrases based on grades 11–12 reading and content, choosing flexibly from a range of strategies.

Materials Needed

- Copies of *Their Eyes Were Watching God* (or alternate assigned text)
- Copies of "In Search of Our Mothers' Gardens" (or alternate assigned text)
- Handout 2.2a: "In Search of Our Mothers' Gardens" Reading Guide
- Handout 2.2b: Quilt Square Explanation
- Handout 2.2c: Quilt Square Template
- A large piece of heavy fabric, cut into evenly sized squares (these can be any size depending on how large you want the final quilt to be; keep in mind that students will need to leave a 1" margin on each side to allow for sewing the squares together)
- A large piece of fabric of the same size to use as the quilt's backing

- Fabric scraps (ask students to bring in old items of clothing and scrap fabric that they find at home; this adds to the collective nature of the project)
- Fabric pens or permanent markers
- Craft glue
- Scissors
- A student/parent volunteer who has a sewing machine and is willing to sew the final quilt together

The Process

After reading *Their Eyes Were Watching God*, students brainstorm about the word "art." What qualifies as art? Why? Who decides what qualifies as art?

Students then read Alice Walker's essay "In Search of Our Mother's Gardens," using a paragraph-by-paragraph annotation guide (Handout 2.2a: "In Search of Our Mothers' Gardens" Reading Guide) that helps them understand Walker's argument that art can be something as seemingly commonplace as a garden or a recipe. At this point, it is important to discuss "high art" (those art forms that are considered to be culturally sophisticated and worthy of study) and "low art" (those art forms that are often unrecognized because of their "common" nature). Ask students what they think the difference between these two forms is and how they think Alice Walker would define each. How does Walker feel about low art? Why does she feel this way?

Students should then learn about the art of quilting and the role that it has played in American culture. The Library of Congress American Memory website (http://www.memory.loc.gov) offers some excellent resources for this, as it contains images of quilts as well as audio interviews with the women who created them. Students could explore quilting on the American Memory website on their own or in groups, or the teacher can create a presentation of the information. In our classes, we created a PowerPoint presentation that includes both audio and visual elements to walk students through a sampling of different quilts.

It is then time to return to a discussion of high and low art. Why would quilting be considered an art? Why would it be considered low art? In reality, to what extent is it accurate to view quilting as a form of low art? In what ways might we see quilting as high art?

At this point, students are ready to begin working on creating their quilt squares. Depending on the size of the class, have students work with partners or in groups of three, and assign each group one or two chapters from the text (again, depending on class size; make sure to cover every chapter of the novel). Student groups need to identify two items: the quotation or passage that they feel is the most important in the chapter, and an image that represents the most important event, theme, or idea in the chapter. Pass out Handout 2.2b: Quilt Square Explanation so they can justify *why* they feel the quotation and image they chose is the most significant in the chapter. Their image can be a literal representation of a key moment (such as Janie learning to shoot a gun) or a symbol that the students create to represent the chapter. Provide students with copies of Handout 2.2c: Quilt Square Template on which to sketch their draft, telling them that they will need to leave a 1" margin on each side of the square to allow for sewing. In order to conserve materials, it is important that students create a preliminary sketch. Students should write the textual evidence they selected along the edges of the square (but still within the 1" margin). Emphasize that they need to choose a passage that is short enough to fit in the allotted space. This gives them practice selecting effective, concise pieces of textual evidence.

Once students have drafted their quilt squares, provide each group with one fabric square per chapter. Provide time for groups to create their images using cuttings from the fabric scraps that they brought in. Students should use fabric pens to write their selected passages around the edges of the square to serve as a border for the image.

Send the completed fabric squares and the fabric backing home with the student or parent who has volunteered to sew the quilt. The finished product is then a collaborative effort, incorporating the work of an entire class into a piece of art that demonstrates students' ability to select key passages from a text, identify main ideas, visualize scenes, and develop original symbols.

Handout 2.2a

"IN SEARCH OF OUR MOTHERS' GARDENS"

Reading Guide

Respond to each of the following questions in the space provided, referring extensively to your copy of "In Search of Our Mothers' Gardens" and making marginal annotations as needed. Be sure to underline or highlight the passages where your find your answers.

Opening poem by Toomer

1. When Toomer says that the prostitute needs a "larger life" for the expression of her nature and temperament, what does he mean?

    _____

    _____

    _____

    _____

    _____

2. What has happened to the emotions of the prostitute?

    _____

    _____

    _____

    _____

    _____

Name: _____ Date: _____

Handout 2.2a: "In Search of Our Mothers' Gardens," continued

3. What does Toomer tell us he has "talked about"?

_____

_____

_____

_____

_____

Paragraph 1

4. Walker addresses the "spirituality" of the Black women that Toomer encountered in the South. What were these women like? What is this "spirituality"? Describe them.

_____

_____

_____

_____

5. How are these Black women treated?

_____

_____

_____

_____

Handout 2.2a: "In Search of Our Mothers' Gardens," continued

6. How does Walker feel about the minds of these women?

_____

_____

_____

_____

_____

Paragraph 4

7. What was the social position of the women of the post-Reconstruction South?

_____

_____

_____

_____

_____

8. What does Walker mean when she tells us that these women "dreamed dreams that no one knew—not even themselves, in any coherent fashion—and saw visions no one could understand"?

_____

_____

_____

_____

_____

Handout 2.2a: "In Search of Our Mothers' Gardens," continued

9. What was the outlet for the dreams of these women?

    _____

    _____

    _____

    _____

    _____

Paragraph 5

10. Why were these women forced to let their minds desert their bodies? What were they giving up?

    _____

    _____

    _____

    _____

    _____

11. If "men lit candles to celebrate the emptiness that remained," what did the men want their women to be?

    _____

    _____

    _____

    _____

    _____

Handout 2.2a: "In Search of Our Mothers' Gardens," continued

Paragraph 6

12. What does Walker mean when she suggests that these women were "moving to music not yet written"?

_____

_____

_____

_____

_____

Paragraph 7

13. How do you know that it will take a very long time for these women to be recognized?

_____

_____

_____

_____

_____

14. Reread the last three sentences of the paragraph. What kind of life would this stifling create for women?

_____

_____

_____

_____

_____

Handout 2.2a: "In Search of Our Mothers' Gardens," continued

Paragraph 8

15. Why were these women's lives so empty?

_____

_____

_____

_____

_____

Paragraph 9

16. According to Walker, what were these women?

_____

_____

_____

_____

_____

17. Why were these women "driven to madness"?

_____

_____

_____

_____

_____

Handout 2.2a: "In Search of Our Mothers' Gardens," continued

Paragraph 11

18. What were these women forced to do?

_____

_____

_____

_____

Paragraph 12

19. Paraphrase the main idea of this paragraph.

_____

_____

_____

_____

Paragraph 13

20. Explain what Walker's altered version of Oko p'Bitek's poem is trying to say.

_____

_____

_____

_____

Handout 2.2a: "In Search of Our Mothers' Gardens," continued

Paragraph 16

21. Walker describes Virginia Woolf's idea that "in order for a woman to write fiction she must have two things, certainly: a room of her own (with key and lock) and enough money to support herself." Why do you think this is?

_____

_____

_____

_____

_____

Paragraph 17

22. How did being Black hinder Phillis Wheatley?

_____

_____

_____

_____

_____

Paragraph 18

23. How does Walker's alteration of Woolf's text emphasize the difficulties facing a Black female artist?

_____

_____

_____

_____

_____

Handout 2.2a: "In Search of Our Mothers' Gardens," continued

Paragraph 19

24. What are the "contrary instincts" that Walker focuses on? What are they a result of?

_____

_____

_____

_____

_____

25. How do you think Phillis Wheatley's mind was "divided"? Why was it divided?

_____

_____

_____

_____

_____

Paragraph 20

26. How did Phillis Wheatley's owners make her reject her heritage?

_____

_____

_____

_____

_____

Handout 2.2a: "In Search of Our Mothers' Gardens," continued

Paragraph 21

27. What was the result of Phillis Wheatley's creative gifts being stifled?

_____

_____

_____

_____

_____

Paragraph 22

28. Why would the excerpt of Wheatley's poem make her seem like a "fool"?

_____

_____

_____

_____

_____

Paragraph 23

29. Where did Wheatley's imagery (or her medium for communicating her gift) come from?

_____

_____

_____

_____

_____

Handout 2.2a: "In Search of Our Mothers' Gardens," continued

Paragraph 25

30. How did Phillis Wheatley keep "alive, in so many of our ancestors, the *notion* of song"?

_____

_____

_____

_____

Paragraph 26

31. What has happened to the image of Black women throughout history?

_____

_____

_____

_____

32. Why do you think that Walker feels that "to be an artist and a Black woman, even today, lowers our status in many respects, rather than raises it: and yet, artists we will be"?

_____

_____

_____

_____

Handout 2.2a: "In Search of Our Mothers' Gardens," continued

Paragraph 30

33. How might the work that Walker's mother needed to do hinder her ability for creative expression?

_____

_____

_____

_____

_____

Paragraph 31

34. Why was/is it so difficult for Black women to create their art?

_____

_____

_____

_____

_____

Paragraph 33

35. Why should we have been looking both "high" and "low" for the art of these women?

_____

_____

_____

_____

_____

Handout 2.2a: "In Search of Our Mothers' Gardens," continued

Paragraph 34

36. How/why is an object like the quilt mentioned in this paragraph just as valuable as (or more valuable than) "high" art?

_____

_____

_____

_____

_____

Paragraph 35

37. What does Walker mean when she discusses "an artist who left her mark in the only materials she could afford, and in the only medium her position in society allowed her to use"?

_____

_____

_____

_____

_____

Paragraph 36

38. What is the main idea of the passage from Virginia Woolf that is included in this paragraph?

_____

_____

_____

_____

Handout 2.2a: "In Search of Our Mothers' Gardens," continued

Paragraph 37

39. How did the mothers and grandmothers "hand on the creative spark"?

_____

_____

_____

_____

_____

Paragraph 38

40. Why does Walker consider her mother's stories a form of art that was passed down to her?

_____

_____

_____

_____

_____

Paragraph 39

41. How does this paragraph emphasize Woolf's idea that, in order for a woman to write fiction, she needs a room of her own and enough money to support herself?

_____

_____

_____

_____

_____

Handout 2.2a: "In Search of Our Mothers' Gardens," continued

Paragraph 40

42. What is Walker's mother's major creative outlet? What is her art?

_____

_____

_____

_____

_____

Paragraph 41

43. Why is her mother's art so important to Walker (what effect did it have on her childhood)?

_____

_____

_____

_____

_____

Paragraph 43

44. How can you tell that the creation of her garden provided a great release/sense of ownership for Walker's mother?

_____

_____

_____

_____

_____

Handout 2.2a: "In Search of Our Mothers' Gardens," continued

Paragraph 45

45. Walker states that "this ability to hold on, even in very simple ways, is work Black women have done for a very long time." How have Black women done this?

_____

_____

_____

_____

_____

Paragraph 46

46. What image of the Black woman is presented in the poem? Who did she take on this role for?

_____

_____

_____

_____

_____

Paragraph 47

47. What do you think Walker means when she says that she found her own garden as she searched for her mother's? What has Walker discovered?

_____

_____

_____

_____

_____

Handout 2.2a: "In Search of Our Mothers' Gardens," continued

Paragraph 50

48. Walker closes the essay by stating that "perhaps in more than Phillis Wheatley's biological life is her mother's signature made clear." Based on the ideas in this essay, how could this be?

_____

_____

_____

_____

_____

_____

_____

_____

_____

_____

Handout 2.2b

QUILT SQUARE EXPLANATION

1. Briefly explain the image on your square. Why have you chosen this image?

_____

_____

_____

_____

_____

_____

_____

_____

2. Explain the significance of the quotation you have chosen to represent the chapter. Why, out of the entire chapter, did you choose this quotation as being the most important one?

_____

_____

_____

_____

_____

_____

_____

_____

Handout 2.2c

QUILT SQUARE TEMPLATE

Sketch your image in the box below. Be sure to include the text that "supports" your image around the edges of the box (remembering that you need to leave a 1" margin on all sides).

MOVIE TRAILER

The creation of movie trailers is perfect in classroom instruction that emphasizes student-centered learning. In the past, this sort of project could take hours of work simply in learning how to use the software, and students weren't able to edit their work. But with new, inexpensive, and easier-to-use technologies, the ability for students to innovate using applications available at most schools is now a reality. In the past few years, the capacity for students to easily produce polished work on film has improved so much that we consistently hear from teachers who gave up on these types of projects years ago. After our encouragement, they have revisited them and are thrilled with the results.

While working in small groups, students are able to enter into a sophisticated and meaningful reading of a full text or selected chapters by creating, through a collaborative effort, a 60-second movie trailer—the type shown in theaters to sell future films. The reason movie trailers are so effective in giving learners a forum in which to delve into thematic connections using textual support is due to their nature. Intended to provide audiences with key details through the selection of important scenes, the editor of the trailer has, in effect, created a visual précis of the movie, replete with theme-building voice-overs and music to reinforce the tone and mood of the piece. The steps of the project are just as academically rich as the final product and can act as microassessments to check for progress in learning objectives. The assignment also encourages revision, which generally occurs in postproduction editing, and may also necessitate refilming certain scenes, or putting in new footage altogether to correct for lack of continuity and flow.

CCSS Alignment

This activity aligns with the following K–12 CCSS in Speaking and Listening.

- CCSS.K-12.SL.1 Comprehension and Collaboration: Prepare for and participate effectively in a range of conversations and collaborations with diverse partners, building on others' ideas and expressing their own clearly and persuasively.

- CCSS.K-12.SL.2 Comprehension and Collaboration: Integrate and evaluate information presented in diverse media and formats, including visually, quantitatively, and orally.
- CCSS.K-12.SL.3 Comprehension and Collaboration: Evaluate a speaker's point of view, reasoning, and use of evidence and rhetoric.
- CCSS.K-12.W.R.5 Production and Distribution of Writing: Develop and strengthen writing as needed by planning, revising, editing, rewriting, or trying a new approach.
- CCSS.K-12.W.R.6 Production and Distribution of Writing: Use technology, including the Internet, to produce and publish writing and to interact and collaborate with others.

Materials Needed

- Student copies of the assigned text
- Video cameras
- Access to computers with video editing software (e.g., Windows Movie Maker, iMovie)

The Process

The steps of the project are fairly simple. Working in small groups, students first create what they consider to be the selling feature of the novel—the central idea that most audiences will find engaging. This central idea acts as a prethematic concept and will serve as a springboard for more sophisticated and challenging ones later in the process.

Once students have a general idea of what they want to say about their piece, they begin to find the key scenes that would reinforce the angle or viewpoint. The group then allocates a scene to each student, who is in charge of creating a script for that scene. The script should include only dialogue from the original, and may include the narrator (who can later be placed into the film as a narrative voice-over). The script should also include the location in which the scene will be filmed. Students meet for a class period to read over the scenes, making any changes and offering suggestions. The filming takes place over the course of a few hours over a weekend or after school.

Students view the first draft of the project by spending one period in a school computer lab. The film is reviewed by the team, and editing changes are made at this point or saved for homework. Musical elements are added to provide an additional layering of the theme. Then, the trailer is viewed by the entire class. The work is assessed in two ways: the process and the final product. We have also had the students, using a class-designed rubric, vote on the top three videos, which are then viewed by another class doing the same project. At the end of the process, the students have created a visual essay and been involved in a project that is both academic and engaging. When students come back to visit us, this is the assignment they remember as being the most meaningful and enjoyable. We have also had several students go into film because of this experience. Strangely, we have never had a student become an essayist because of the number of challenging essays we assign!

There are several iterations of the assignment. We have had students create movie trailers from the point of view of a different character from the original work. Third-person narratives can be reimagined as first-person confessionals. Scenes that weren't included in the novel are added in an assignment we call *Missing Footage*, with a voice-over explaining why this piece is so important to our understanding of the novel as a whole. We have had students add a 30-second commercial in the center of their work to sell a product that would have been used during the time period in which the novel takes place. If the novel is historically accurate, this addition would require some fast research. If the novel is science fiction, the addition is merely creative.

ALLEGORY

We have all watched students struggling with complex texts, especially something as complex as an allegory. This is an activity that can be completed in one or two class periods. While we have used it with Plato's "Allegory of the Cave" (360 B.C.E.), it can be used with any allegory, such as Hawthorne's "Young Goodman Brown" (1835), or even an excerpt from a longer piece.

This activity is also an effective formative assessment, providing the teacher with an easy way to see whether students are grasping the literal meaning of a text as well as its underlying allegorical meaning.

CCSS Alignment

This activity addresses the following CCSS. Because the suggested text, Plato's "Allegory of the Cave," is in the senior curriculum, the standards listed are those for grades 11 and 12.

- CCSS.11-12.R.L.1 Key Ideas and Details: Cite strong and thorough textual evidence to support analysis of what the text says explicitly as well as inferences drawn from the text, including determining where the text leaves matters uncertain.
- CCSS.11-12.R.L.2 Key Ideas and Details: Determine two or more themes or central ideas of a text and analyze their development over the course of the text, including how they interact and build on one another to produce a complex account; provide an objective summary of the text.
- CCSS.11-12.R.L.10 Range of Reading and Level of Text Complexity: By the end of grade 11, read and comprehend literature, including stories, dramas, and poems, in the grades 11–12 CCR text complexity band proficiently, with scaffolding as needed at the high end of the range. By the end of grade 12, read and comprehend literature, including stories, dramas, and poems, at the high end of the grades 11–12 CCR text complexity band independently and proficiently.
- CCSS.11-12.SL.1 Comprehension and Collaboration: Initiate and participate effectively in a range of collaborative discussions (one-on-one, in groups, and teacher-led) with diverse partners on grades

11–12 topics, texts, and issues, building on others' ideas and expressing their own clearly and persuasively.

Materials Needed

- Student copies of Plato's "Allegory of the Cave" (or alternate assigned text)
- Large pieces of paper (either large copy paper or butcher paper will work)
- Colored pencils or markers

The Process

With this activity, it is best to give the students as little information ahead of time as possible. For example, you can pass out a copy of "Allegory of the Cave" with no title or author on it, so that students do not have any frame of reference for what they are about to read.

The first step of the process is for students to read the text aloud in small groups, summarizing the story in the margins. It is important to emphasize that they are only to focus on the narrative line of the story at this point, and that they are not to concern themselves with meaning. Once they have completed a preliminary reading, pass out large pieces of paper and instruct students to draw what they have read in comic strip form, strictly using images without words. As the teacher circulates the room during this phase, it is easy to see how clearly students understand the literal level of the text and to identify and intervene in any groups that show misunderstanding or struggle.

Once students have completed their comic strips, it is time to talk about allegory. Along with a formal definition, we always like to explain allegory by drawing a simple sketch on the board of a person walking down a street, away from his house and into the forest. We explain to students that this is the literal level of the story; this is what they have already identified. Then, we erase the line that represents the ground and explain that when reading an allegory, we essentially pull the ground out from under the literal level and delve below the surface in order to uncover meaning. At this point, it is also important to discuss elements like symbols and colors and the role these play in making meaning out of an allegory. At this point, you might reveal the title of the piece that students are reading. In some cases, knowing the title will help students to create meaning, but this is not always true. If this is the first time that a group is working with allegory in your class, you might consider telling students what the piece is an allegory for; this way the focus is on close reading and identification of symbols and their function, as opposed to trying to guess the "right answer" of what the piece is about.

Students then return to the text and to their comic strips. As they reread the text and follow the progression of the plot on their comic strips, they begin to write captions for each panel that explain the allegorical significance of what is taking place. At this point, students should also be identifying elements like archetypal symbols and commenting on how they contribute to the meaning of the allegory.

The final product is a completed comic strip that consists of images and panels (see Figures 12–14). Student groups can present their work, or they can hang them on the walls and participate in a "gallery walk," moving around the room and examining each comic, noting how each interpretation adds to or changes their understanding of the text. A follow-up discussion can revolve around noting the differences in interpretation that the various groups have, which, in turn, leads to a rich discussion of the text itself.

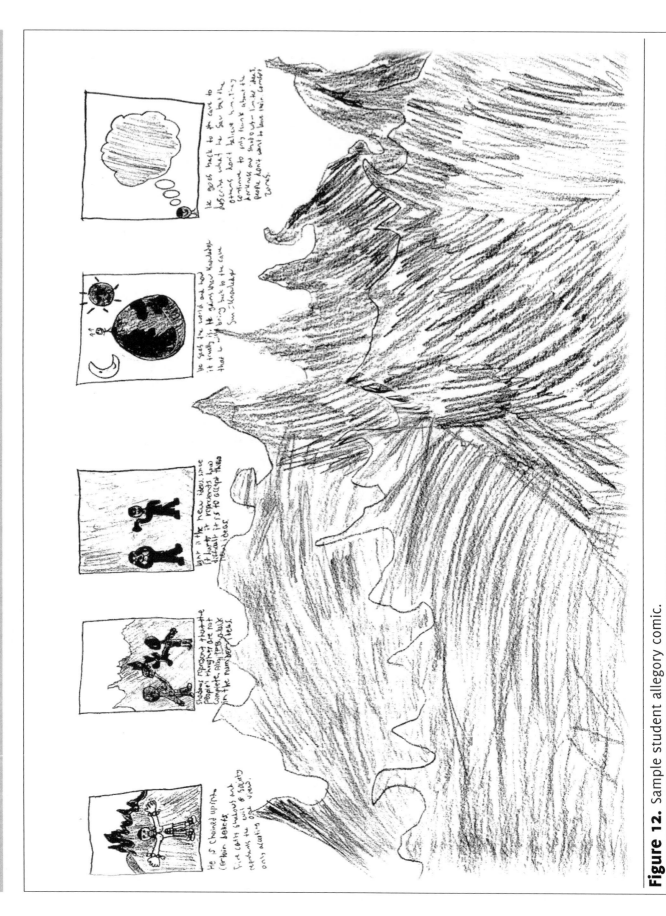

Figure 12. Sample student allegory comic.

Figure 13. Sample student allegory comic.

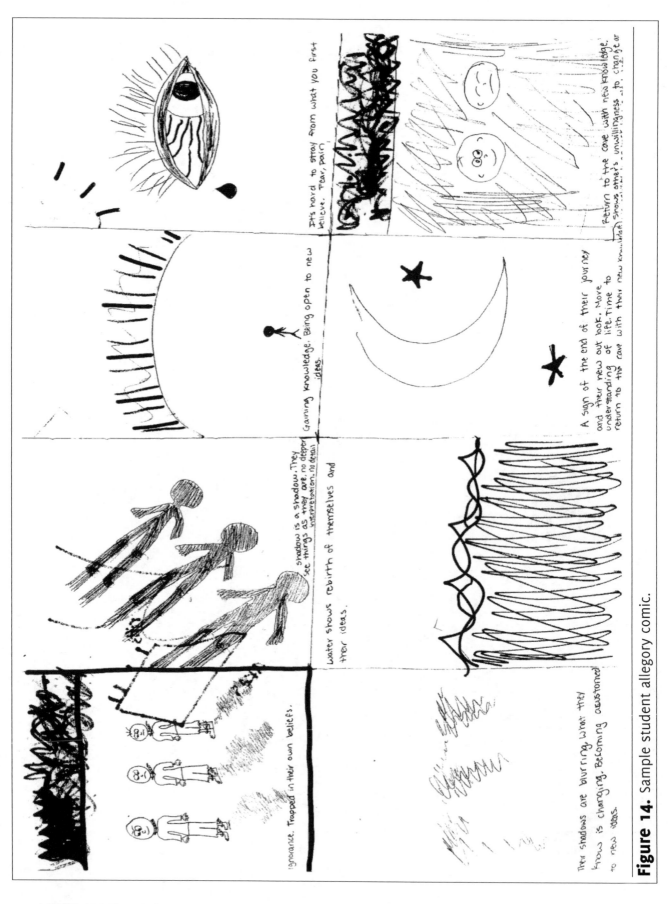

Figure 14. Sample student allegory comic.

Chapter 3

DECONSTRUCTION

The activities in this chapter demonstrate a student's ability to transfer lower level skills to the highest level of critical thinking. The student-driven analysis provides for choice, engagement, differentiation, and intrinsic motivation. Students choose the focus of their textual analysis and create a visual or auditory analogy of the author's choices. The student-driven creation of the analysis exhibits the student's ability to closely read, construct, and show their own patterns of judgment and thinking. Once students have mastered this level, they are able to transfer these skills to a myriad of complex texts.

As with all of the activities in this book, the activities from this chapter can be adapted for a number of texts. Activity 3.1: The Soundtrack is suggested for use with *Ordinary People* (Guest, 1982). Activity 3.2 can be used with any text. We like to use *The Things They Carried* (O'Brien, 1990/2009).

Activity 3.1:

THE SOUNDTRACK

For many students, music is an integral part of their daily lives. Besides providing sheer enjoyment, music has the potential to comfort someone who is sad, relax someone who is stressed, and invigorate someone who needs energy or focus. In short, many students have a deep connection to their playlists because they are personal.

Because so many students can relate to artists' lyrics, having students create a playlist for a text is a natural extension of literature. This activity can be modified for any piece of literature and can either be extended or truncated to fit the situation. Even weaker students tend to do well when asked to use music as part of a writing activity because they are more invested in the assignment. Because there is also an element of art to this project, students who have an artistic bent enjoy creating their own cover art for the CD. This is multimodal learning, and students do not disappoint in demonstrating how well they understand the novel.

CCSS Alignment

Using *Ordinary People* as a 10th-grade text, this project addresses the following CCSS for grades 9 and 10.

- CCSS.9-10.R.L.1 Key Ideas and Details: Cite strong and thorough textual evidence to support analysis of what the text says explicitly as well as inferences drawn from the text.
- CCSS.9-10.R.L.10 Range of Reading and Level of Text Complexity: By the end of grade 9, read and comprehend literature, including stories, dramas, and poems, in the grades 9–10 text complexity band proficiently, with scaffolding as needed at the high end of the range. By the end of grade 10, read and comprehend literature, including stories, dramas, and poems, at the high end of the grades 9–10 text complexity band independently and proficiently.
- CCSS.9-10.W.4 Production and Distribution of Writing: Produce clear and coherent writing in which the development, organization, and style are appropriate to task, purpose, and audience. (Grade-specific expectations for writing types are defined in standards 1–3 above.)

- CCSS.9-10.SL.1 Comprehension and Collaboration: Initiate and participate effectively in a range of collaborative discussions (one-on-one, in groups, and teacher-led) with diverse partners on grades 9–10 topics, texts, and issues, building on others' ideas and expressing their own clearly and persuasively.
- CCSS.9-10.SL.5 Presentation of Knowledge and Ideas: Make strategic use of digital media (e.g., textual, graphical, audio, visual, and interactive elements) in presentations to enhance understanding of findings, reasoning, and evidence and to add interest.

Materials Needed

- Student copies of *Ordinary People* (or alternate assigned text)
- Access to media player (e.g., iTunes)
- Drawing or painting supplies, or access to design software (e.g., InDesign)

The Process

Rather than writing a paper for *Ordinary People* (Guest, 1982), students are going to create a soundtrack for the book. (Yes, the novel has been made into a movie, but the music is limited and lacks lyrics.) Although the novel has 32 chapters (31 plus an epilogue), students have the choice of working alone or with a partner. The goal of the assignment is to choose 12 songs from various musical artists and match them to specific chapters. Students will create a soundtrack for the novel.

Students may choose to highlight any 12 chapters, or they may choose specific events throughout the novel and highlight those events. (Have students scatter their chapters; they should not choose the first 12 chapters or the last 12 chapters.) Regardless of whether students choose chapters or events, they must list the chapters with a brief summary or highlight the specific events with a brief explanation, and explain why the song fits so well (see Figure 15). Moreover, students should include textual evidence from the both the novel and the lyrics. Remind them to cite appropriately, using MLA format.

> Chapter 1: In this chapter, the reader meets Conrad Jarrett, a high school junior. The story opens with the comment, "To get up in the morning, it is necessary to possess a guiding principle" (Guest 1). Conrad is lying in bed, pondering the changes that have been made to his bedroom. The reader learns that he has been hospitalized in the past and has been home a month. In addition, it is evident that Conrad is anxious and has difficulty making decisions. In fact, little things from what to wear to brushing his teeth seem to overwhelm him and he cannot relax. Nonetheless, he somehow manages to pull it together and get ready for school.
>
> Song Title: "Everybody Hurts" by REM from *Automatic for the People.*
>
> Rationale: This song is a perfect fit for chapter one because it reinforces Conrad's feelings that life is difficult. In the opening stanza, the lyrics read, "When the day is long and the night . . . is yours alone,/When you're sure that you've had enough of this life, well hang on/Don't let yourself go, 'cause everybody cries and everybody hurts/sometimes." The reader learns that Conrad's state of mind is fragile and that he is unsure whether he can make it through the simple tasks of the day: getting out of bed, washing his face, brushing his teeth, and getting dressed. Life totally overwhelms him. Like the song's lyrics, though, Conrad knows to " . . . hold on, hold on . . . [because he is] not alone."

Figure 15. Sample chapter summary and explanation.

After compiling the soundtrack, students will design an original CD cover that represents the novel as a whole. Consider the following ideas for depictions on a CD cover:

- A main character's development (Conrad, Calvin, Beth, or Berger)
- Another character's development (Karen, Lazenby, Stillman, Salan, or Jeannine)
- Primary conflicts (internal and/or external) in the novel that capture thoughts, feelings, and emotions
- Any resolutions or solutions to the internal and/or external conflicts
- The setting of the story
- Any "aha" moment in the story
- Any themes, symbols, or motifs
- Mood or tone

The completed project will include the following elements: a list of songs related to *Ordinary People*, a cover for the CD, and the page that clearly summarizes the specific chapters/events, includes a thorough rationale for each song chosen, and properly cites text and lyrics. On the day the project is due, each student or group should share one of the chosen songs with the class.

THE ART OF REDUCTION

Perhaps the idea of reducing something stirs up negative connotations. But asking students to reduce a text provides a clear assessment of their ability to analyze text, literary or informational.

Although English teachers do ask students to analyze literary and informational text in the classroom, we often combine essay writing with analysis. This can become confusing for students and teachers in relation to assessment. What exactly are we assessing when we ask students to write a literary analysis? Their reading comprehension and analysis, writing skills, or both?

It may benefit us, as well as our students, to clearly separate the two skills. In turn, we are creating formative assessment that clearly identifies student's composition and reading skill strengths and deficits. We can approach this method through the assessment we call a reduction.

In cooking, reduction is the process of thickening or intensifying the flavor of a liquid mixture such as soup, sauce, wine, or juice through evaporation. The goal is to increase the flavor while boiling away the unnecessary ingredients. The technique of cooking liquids down to cause the unnecessary water to evaporate intensifies the flavor.

In the study of literature, the reduction is the "boiling down" of text in order for the students to create a synthesis of concentrated ideas through the analysis. The reduction becomes the intensified "flavor" that emerges from the reading and discussion of the text. Through the creation of the reduction, students move to what Kelley Gallagher (2004) refers to as the "why does it matter?" stage (p. 89). Once students can summarize text and indicate the meaning, ask them to tell you why it matters. Moving students to the phase of why it matters brings them to practice and master the important lifelong skill of critical thinking.

Although the main purpose of the reduction is to ask students to analyze text critically, the other wonderful aspect of the reduction assignment is that it is completely student-driven. When you assign reductions, you share the assessment at the beginning of the novel, poem, or essay. In assigning the task, ask students to focus on one area. They should choose one of the following to guide their reading:

- author,
- title,

- setting,
- character(s),
- diction and syntax,
- structure of the entire work, or
- literary devices: irony, etc.

Ask students to conduct a close reading as they navigate the text. This is different from an essay. Their reduction could eventually become an essay, but it does not have to. The benefit here is that you can formatively assess students' analyses prior to their synthesis and argument. This approach helps the students revise erroneous or nonfocused thinking prior to writing down their argument. You can work with the students to troubleshoot and correct potential places of misguided or off-topic analysis.

CCSS Alignment

The CCSS identify the area of textual analysis as an integral component for college readiness. The Common Core identifies anchor standards in the areas of reading, writing, and speaking and listening. In the area of reading, the anchor standards for Key Ideas and Details state:

- CCSS.ELA-Literacy.CCRA.R.1 Read closely to determine what the text says explicitly and to make logical inferences from it; cite specific textual evidence when writing or speaking to support conclusions drawn from the text.
- CCSS.ELA-Literacy.CCRA.R.2 Determine central ideas or themes of a text and analyze their development; summarize the key supporting details and ideas.
- CCSS.ELA-Literacy.CCRA.R.3 Analyze how and why individuals, events, or ideas develop and interact over the course of a text.

Materials Needed

- Student copies of assigned text
- Drawing instruments or Internet access (to find a premade visual)
- Handout 3.2: Student Note-Taking

The Process

The first time you ask students to complete a reduction, provide them with salient passages from the text. Students should have already read the entire text, and you should have assessed literal comprehension and cleared up any plot-based confusion. Once you have completed this important step, students are ready to begin their analysis. As you can see in the CCSS, in the area of reading, students need to show that they can "Determine central ideas or themes of a text and analyze their development; summarize the key supporting details and ideas. And analyze how and why individuals, events, or ideas develop and interact over the course of a text." Reading standards 1 and 10 encompass all other reading standards. Therefore, through the task of reducing the text, you can specifically assess standards 2 and 3.

When assigning a reduction, ask students to choose, and reread, one of any number of predetermined passages. Ask students what their passage "looks like." At this point, students can think literally or metaphorically. The visualization step is integral to the creation of the reduction. With the knowledge that approximately 80% of students are visual learners, this is a vital step in their analysis. Although you may not teach a visual arts class, you do need to know how students perceive the text.

During the visualization, you may wish to provide your students with access to the Internet. This will help students who do not feel comfortable drawing determine how they see the passage. Once students have a visual, ask them to pull an excerpt from the text to support their image. At this point, some students also support their visual assertion with other areas of the text. Encourage students who can do so to make the larger connections, but do not require it of all students.

In Figure 16, the student embellished the salient passage with his visual interpretation. At this point, it is very acceptable for students to be at a literal visualization level. We eventually lead students to the analogy or metaphorical representation. Students present their analysis of the scene via a museum walk.

Once the salient scene reduction is complete, ask students to display their reductions. You can conduct a "Pictures at an Exhibition" session and have students individually present their analyses. This museum walk or presentation can be held prior to the test or final essay. This will allow students to review the entire novel prior to the summative assessment. While students observe each other's analyses, ask them to complete Handout 3.2: Student Note-Taking. You can ask students to respond to this question either as

Figure 16. Sample student reduction.

homework or as a timed writing assessment. Therefore, students are using each other's analyses to inform their own analysis of the novel.

At the end of the review (either one or 2 days), students will have a review guide of the entire novel, they will have identified appropriate quotations, and they will have an analysis of the text. They have gathered all of the evidence they need in order to write an effective argument of the text.

Although you should begin this process with a smaller-scale scaffold approach using salient scenes, eventually you can ask students to reduce the entire novel to one page. Again, this is not to trivialize or minimize the text, but rather to guide student analysis of the salient pieces of the text. On the first day of studying the novel, ask students to choose an area of annotated focus. You can allow students to choose any area on the first reduction, even an area they have fully mastered in the past. This helps students focus on the text rather than on understanding the skill of character analysis, for example. As the year progresses, you can repeat the reduction assignment with each major work. During the later reductions, ask students to choose a different area of focus.

For example, when our high school juniors read *The Things They Carried*, we had them randomly choose one of six characters: Tim O'Brien, Norman Bowker, Kiowa, Jimmy Cross, Henry Dobbins, or Mitchell Sanders. We read the first chapter together after students received their character. We asked students only to highlight what their assigned character carried, including both concrete carries and abstract carries. As students continued to read the novel, their focus of annotating was only on their character. In working through the focused annotations, we avoided formulaic annotations, disruption of fluency, and overannotation.

With this particular novel, we asked students to read it straight through. We had no classroom activities during the reading. We determined that the plot was easily accessible and needed minimal teacher guidance; therefore, we knew students could manage the reading/comprehension of the text. We also carved out in-class reading time, and we did not "quiz" our students on, for example, Chapters 1–3 on Monday and 4–7 on Wednesday.

At the completion of the reading, students began to work on their visualization of character. How did they see their character? At this point, some students visualize concretely and others begin to challenge themselves with the abstract. We allowed students to choose their visualization in order to create a differentiated and equitable assessment. We asked students to be aware of how they placed their analysis on the page. Everything on the one page reduction must have meaning: layout, font style, and size, as well as color and images. One note of caution: Students should focus more on text than an image.

The student who created the reduction in Figure 17 was beginning to move from literal representation to the metaphorical. She placed the "comfortable things the soldiers carry" in the house. She placed the uncomfortable things the soldiers carry outside of the house. Her analysis focuses on all of the carries but creates a classification system for them. She also shared how there are carries we accept, carries that are safe, and then there are carries that are imposed upon us. The placement of the text either inside the house or outside the house supports the metaphor of a home or households. Home is safe and comfortable. Outside of the home is the unknown and the feared.

Figure 18 shows critical, complex analysis of text. The student understood that O'Brien's purpose in writing the novel was not to share the horrors of war, but rather to keep memories alive. Ryan read an excerpt from a Tim O'Brien lecture that shared O'Brien's belief of "happening truth vs. story truth." He used this premise to govern his analysis. The overall image of the gun's scope reinforces the idea of O'Brien's focus: the elusive yet embellished truth. Through Figure 17, we see the student's analysis of the character Tim O'Brien. The student has created an assertion about the novel and has gathered his evidence. He is ready to write his literary argument.

As you can see with these examples, each reduction is different; each is student-driven, and each is an analysis of text. With the nationwide movement to the CCSS, we need to be certain that students are mastering spe-

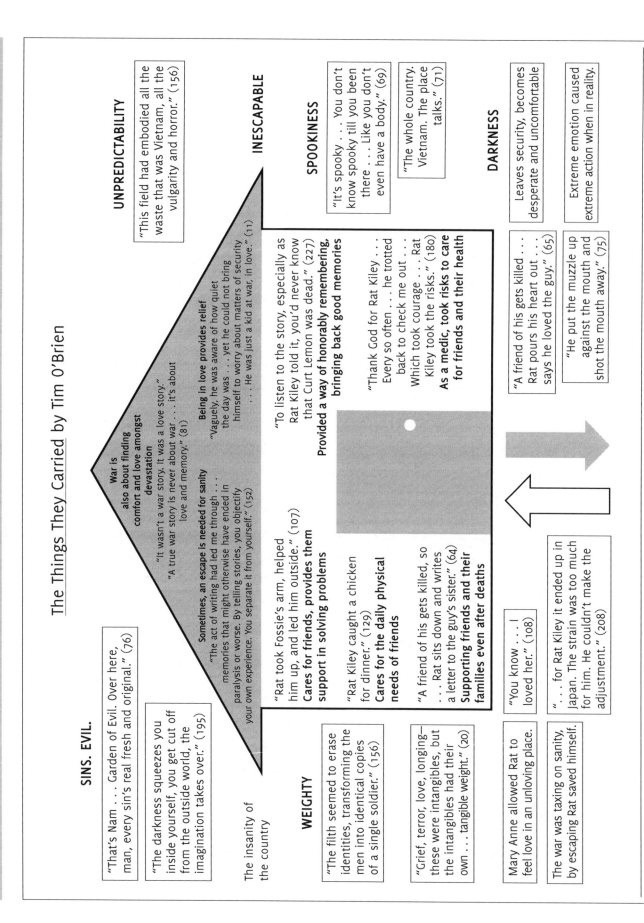

The Things They Carried by Tim O'Brien

UNPREDICTABILITY

"This field had embodied all the waste that was Vietnam, all the vulgarity and horror." (156)

INESCAPABLE

SPOOKINESS

"It's spooky . . . You don't know how spooky till you been there . . . Like you don't even have a body." (69)

"The whole country. Vietnam. The place talks." (71)

DARKNESS

Leaves security, becomes desperate and uncomfortable

Extreme emotion caused extreme action when in reality.

SINS. EVIL.

"That's Nam . . . Garden of Evil. Over here, man, every sin's real fresh and original." (76)

"The darkness squeezes you inside yourself, you get cut off from the outside world, the imagination takes over." (195)

The insanity of the country

War is also about finding comfort and love amongst devastation

"It wasn't a war story. It was a love story." "A true war story is never about war . . . it's about love and memory." (81)

Being in love provides relief

"Vaguely, he was aware of how quiet the day was . . . yet he could not bring himself to worry about matters of security . . . He was just a kid at war, in love." (11)

Sometimes, an escape is needed for sanity

"The act of writing had led me through . . . memories that might otherwise have ended in paralysis or worse. By telling stories, you objectify your own experience. You separate it from yourself." (152)

"To listen to the story, especially as Rat Kiley told it, you'd never know that Curt Lemon was dead." (227)

Provided a way of honorably remembering, bringing back good memories

"Thank God for Rat Kiley . . . Every so often . . . he trotted back to check me out . . . Which took courage . . . Rat Kiley took the risks." (180)

As a medic, took risks to care for friends and their health

"A friend of his gets killed . . . Rat pours his heart out . . . says he loved the guy." (65)

"He put the muzzle up against the mouth and shot the mouth away." (75)

WEIGHTY

"The filth seemed to erase identities, transforming the men into identical copies of a single soldier." (156)

"Grief, terror, love, longing—these were intangibles, but the intangibles had their own . . . tangible weight." (20)

Mary Anne allowed Rat to feel love in an unloving place.

The war was taxing on sanity, by escaping Rat saved himself.

"Rat took Fossie's arm, helped him up, and led him outside." (107)

Cares for friends, provides them support in solving problems

"Rat Kiley caught a chicken for dinner." (129)

Cares for the daily physical needs of friends

"A friend of his gets killed, so . . . Rat sits down and writes a letter to the guy's sister." (64)

Supporting friends and their families even after deaths

"You know . . . I loved her." (108)

". . . for Rat Kiley it ended up in Japan. The strain was too much for him. He couldn't make the adjustment." (208)

Figure 17. Student visual reduction of *The Things They Carried*.

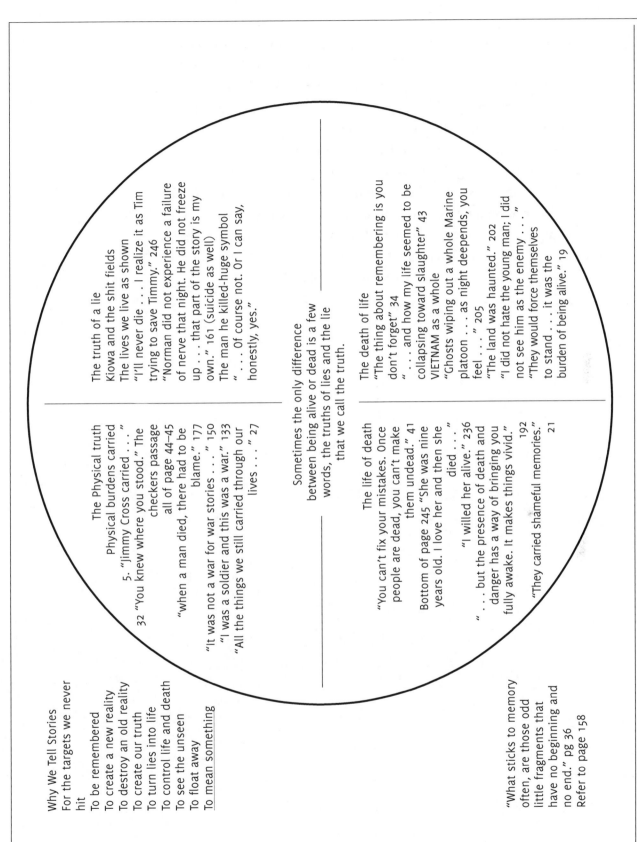

Figure 18. Student visual reduction of *The Things They Carried.*

cific, explicit skills. The reduction teases out analysis from written argument. Although the assessment could be considered summative, because it does assess the students' reading ability, it also serves as a formative assessment prior to an essay or test. If you choose to follow the reduction with a test, the focus of the test should be analysis of text. Provide your students, ahead of the assessment, with a new test. During the assessment, focus on the analysis of the text answering the question of "Why does it matter?"

The reduction is a recurring assignment in our classroom throughout the year. We assess students using the same rubric each time and ask students to complete Handout 3.2: Student Note-Taking each time. This serves two purposes: Students as well as the teacher can chart student growth toward mastery, and students have their notes to review for the final exam.

Name: _____ Date: _____

_____

STUDENT NOTE-TAKING

While your classmates present their reductions, you will take notes. While listening to reductions, you will be able to:

- identify recurring motifs (objects that are repeated),
- identify recurring thematic concepts that appear in the text,
- connect other's analyses to your understanding of the novel and other readings, and
- explain why the analyses matter.

Student Name	Reduction Focus: What Is the Student Trying to prove?	Motifs	Thematic Concepts	Conclusions: Why Does This Matter?

How do the analyses presented today enhance your understanding of the novel?

_____

_____

_____

_____

_____

_____

_____

_____

_____

REFERENCES

Bradbury, R. (2012). *Fahrenheit 451*. New York, NY: Simon & Schuster. (Original work published 1953)

Brontë, C. (2000). *Jane Eyre*. New York, NY: W. W. Norton & Company. (Original work published 1847)

Fitzgerald, F. S. (2004). *The Great Gatsby*. New York, NY: Scribner. (Original work published 1925)

Gallagher, K. (2004). *Deeper reading: Comprehending challenging texts, 4–12*. Portland, ME: Stenhouse.

Guest, J. (1982). *Ordinary people*. New York, NY: Penguin.

Hawthorne, N. (1835). *Young Goodman Brown* [Literature Network version]. Retrieved from http://www.online-literature.com/poe/158/

Hoess, R. (1946). *Testimony of Rudolf Hoess, Commandant of Auschwitz*. Retrieved from http://law2.umkc.edu/faculty/projects/ftrials/nuremberg/hoesstest.html

Hsu, H. (2009, January). The end of white America? *The Atlantic*. Retrieved from http://www.theatlantic.com/magazine/archive/2009/01/the-end-of-white-america/307208/

Hurston, Z. N. (2006). *Their eyes were watching God*. New York, NY: Harper Perennial. (Original work published 1937)

Milgram, S. (1974). *Obedience to authority: An experimental view*. New York, NY: Harper and Row.

O'Brien, T. (2009). *The things they carried*. New York, NY: Mariner Books. (Original work published 1990)

Plato. (360 B.C.E.). Book VII. In *The Republic* (B. Jowett, Trans.). Retrieved from http://classics.mit.edu/Plato/republic.8.vii.html

Salinger, J. D. (1991). *The catcher in the rye.* New York, NY: Little, Brown. (Original work published 1951)

Schmelling, S. (2009). *Ophelia joined the group, Maidens Who Don't Float: Classic lit signs on to Facebook.* New York, NY: Plume.

Thoreau, H. D. (2009). *Civil disobedience* [Thoreau Reader version]. Retrieved from http://thoreau.eserver.org/civil.html (Original work published 1849)

Walker, A. (2002). In search of our mothers' gardens: The creativity of Black women in the south. *Ms. Magazine.* Retrieved from http://www.msmagazine.com/spring2002/walker.asp (Original work published 1974)

APPENDIX: SUGGESTED READINGS

Chapter 1: Understanding

Activity 1.1:

FRIENDING FACEBOOK IN THE CLASSROOM

12 Angry Men, Reginald Rose

The Canterbury Tales, Geoffrey Chaucer

Extremely Loud and Incredibly Close, Jonathan Safran Foer

Fahrenheit 451, Ray Bradbury

The Great Gatsby, F. Scott Fitzgerald

My Sister's Keeper, Jodi Picoult

A Tale of Two Cities, Charles Dickens

The Tortilla Curtain, T. C. Boyle

VISUALIZING TEXT

"Civil Disobedience," Henry David Thoreau
"Letter From Birmingham Jail," Martin Luther King, Jr.
Narrative of the Life of Frederick Douglass, Frederick Douglass
Presidential Inaugural Addresses
"Testimony of Rudolf Hoess, Commandant of Auschwitz"

Chapter 2: Adaptation

Activity 2.1:

GRAPHIC NOVEL

The Body, Stephen King
Extremely Loud and Incredibly Close, Jonathan Safran Foer
Hamlet, William Shakespeare
The House on Mango Street, Sandra Cisneros
Macbeth, William Shakespeare
The Plague, Albert Camus
Romeo and Juliet, William Shakespeare

Activity 2.2:

QUILT AS HIGH ART

The Color Purple, Alice Walker
"In Search of Our Mothers' Gardens," Alice Walker
Mama Day, Gloria Naylor
Their Eyes Were Watching God, Zora Neale Hurston

Activity 2.3:
MOVIE TRAILER

1984, George Orwell
Jane Eyre, Charlotte Brontë
Lord of the Flies, William Golding
To Kill a Mockingbird, Harper Lee

Activity 2.4:
ALLEGORY

"Allegory of the Cave" in *The Republic,* Plato
Animal Farm, George Orwell
Inferno, opening canto, Dante Alighieri
"Young Goodman Brown," Nathaniel Hawthorne

Chapter 3: Deconstruction

Activity 3.1:
THE SOUNDTRACK

The Great Gatsby, F. Scott Fitzgerald
Hamlet, William Shakespeare
King Lear, William Shakespeare
Macbeth, William Shakespeare
Ordinary People, Judith Guest
Othello, William Shakespeare
Romeo and Juliet, William Shakespeare

THE ART OF REDUCTION

East of Eden, John Steinbeck

Ella Minnow Pea, Mark Dunn

Fahrenheit 451, Ray Bradbury

The Great Gatsby, F. Scott Fitzgerald

"Harrison Bergeron," Kurt Vonnegut

To Kill a Mockingbird, Harper Lee

A Lesson Before Dying, Ernest J. Gaines

Lord of the Flies, William Golding

A Passage to India, E. M. Forster

Pride and Prejudice, Jane Austen

The Scarlet Letter, Nathaniel Hawthorne

Things Fall Apart, Chinua Achebe

The Things They Carried, Tim O'Brien

ABOUT THE AUTHORS

Beth Ahlgrim is the English Department Chair at Deerfield High School in Deerfield, IL. Beth earned her master's degree in English literature from DePaul University and her master's in educational leadership from Northeastern Illinois University.

Bill Fritz has more than 25 years of teaching experience. He served in the Peace Corps and taught English as a Second Language to Berbers in Morocco before attaining a master's degree in education from Northwestern University. He currently teaches English at Adlai E. Stevenson High School in Lincolnshire, IL, and was named a finalist for Illinois Teacher of the Year by the Illinois State Board of Education in 2013.

Jeremy Gertzfield taught English at Adlai E. Stevenson High School in Lincolnshire, IL, for 12 years before relocating to Shanghai American School in Shanghai, China. He holds a master's degree in English from Roosevelt University.

Lisa Lukens has more than 20 years of experience teaching English. She holds a master's of education degree in curriculum and instruction from Loyola University-Chicago. She currently teaches at Adlai E. Stevenson High School in Lincolnshire, IL.

COMMON CORE
STATE STANDARDS
ALIGNMENT

Menu	Common Core State Standards
	Chapter 1: Understanding
Activity 1.1: Friending Facebook in the Classroom	CCSS.ELA-Literacy.SL1b Work with peers to promote civil, democratic discussions and decision-making, set clear goals and deadlines, and establish individual roles as needed.
	CCSS.ELA-Literacy.RL.1 Cite strong and thorough textual evidence to support analysis of what the text says explicitly as well as inferences drawn from the text, including determining where the text leaves matters uncertain.
	CCSS.ELA-Literacy.RL.2 Determine two or more themes or central ideas of a text and analyze their development over the course of the text, including how they interact and build on one another to produce a complex account; provide an objective summary of the text.
	CCSS.ELA-Literacy.RL.3 Analyze the impact of the author's choices regarding how to develop and relate elements of a story or drama (e.g., where a story is set, how the action is ordered, how the characters are introduced and developed).
	CCSS.ELA-Literacy.RI.3 Analyze a complex set of ideas or sequence of events and explain how specific individuals, ideas, or events interact and develop over the course of the text.
	CCSS.ELA-Literacy.SL.1c Propel conversations by posing and responding to questions that probe reasoning and evidence; ensure a hearing for a full range of positions on a topic or issue; clarify, verify, or challenge ideas and conclusions; and promote divergent and creative perspectives.

Menu	Common Core State Standards
Activity 1.1: Friending Facebook in the Classroom, *continued*	CCSS.ELA-Literacy.SL.1d Respond thoughtfully to diverse perspectives; synthesize comments, claims, and evidence made on all sides of an issue; resolve contradictions when possible; and determine what additional information or research is required to deepen the investigation or complete the task.
	CCSS.ELA-Literacy.SL5 Make strategic use of digital media (e.g., textual, graphical, audio, visual, and interactive elements) in presentations to enhance understanding of findings, reasoning, and evidence and to add interest.
Activity 1.2: Visualizing Text	CCSS.ELA-Literacy.RI.9-10.2: Determine a central idea of a text and analyze its development over the course of the text, including how it emerges and is shaped and refined by specific details; provide an objective summary of the text.
	CCSS.ELA-Literacy.RI.9-10.4: Determine the meaning of words and phrases as they are used in a text, including figurative, connotative, and technical meanings; analyze the cumulative impact of specific word choices on meaning and tone (e.g., how the language of a court opinion differs from that of a newspaper).
	CCSS.ELA-Literacy.RI.9-10.5: Analyze in detail how an author's ideas or claims are developed and refined by particular sentences, paragraphs, or larger portions of a text (e.g., a section or chapter).
	CCSS.ELA-Literacy.RI.9-10.6: Determine an author's point of view or purpose in a text and analyze how an author uses rhetoric to advance that point of view or purpose.
	CCSS.ELA-Literacy.RI.9-10.8: Delineate and evaluate the argument and specific claims in a text, assessing whether the reasoning is valid and the evidence is relevant and sufficient; identify false statements and fallacious reasoning.
	CCSS.ELA-Literacy.W.9-10.1a: Introduce precise claim(s), distinguish the claim(s) from alternate or opposing claims, and create an organization that establishes clear relationships among claim(s), counterclaims, reasons, and evidence.
	CCSS.ELA-Literacy.W.9-10.1c: Use words, phrases, and clauses to link the major sections of the text, create cohesion, and clarify the relationships between claim(s) and reasons, between reasons and evidence, and between claim(s) and counterclaims.
	CCSS.ELA-Literacy.W.9-10.1d: Establish and maintain a formal style and objective tone while attending to the norms and conventions of the discipline in which they are writing.
	CCSS.ELA-Literacy.W.9-10.1e: Provide a concluding statement or section that follows from and supports the argument presented.

Menu	Common Core State Standards
Activity 1.2: Visualizing Text, *continued*	CCSS.ELA-Literacy.SL.9-10.4: Present information, findings, and supporting evidence clearly, concisely, and logically such that listeners can follow the line of reasoning and the organization, development, substance, and style are appropriate to purpose and task.
	CCSS.ELA-Literacy.SL.9-10.5: Make strategic use of digital media (e.g., textual, graphical, audio, visual, and interactive elements) in presentations to enhance understanding of findings, reasoning, and evidence and to add interest.
Chapter 2: Adaptation	
Activity 2.1: Graphic Novel	CCSS.ELA-Literacy.K-12.SL.2 Comprehension and Collaboration: Integrate and evaluate information presented in diverse media and formats, including visually, quantitatively, and orally.
	CCSS.ELA-Literacy.K-12.SL.3 Comprehension and Collaboration: Evaluate a speaker's point of view, reasoning, and use of evidence and rhetoric.
	CCSS.ELA-Literacy.K-12 R.2 Key Ideas and Details: Determine central ideas or themes of a text and analyze their development; summarize the key supporting details and ideas.
	CCSS.ELA-Literacy.K-12.R.R.3 Key Ideas and Details: Analyze how and why individuals, events, and ideas develop and interact over the course of a text.
	CCSS.ELA-Literacy.K-12.R.R.4 Craft and Structure: Interpret words and phrases as they are used in a text, including determining technical, connotative, and figurative meanings, and analyze how specific word choices shape meaning or tone.
	CCSS.ELA-Literacy.K-12.R.R.5 Craft and Structure: Analyze the structure of texts, including how specific sentences, paragraphs, and larger portions of the text (e.g., a section, chapter, scene, or stanza) relate to each other and the whole.
	CCSS.ELA-Literacy.K-12.R.R.6 Craft and Structure: Assess how point of view or purpose shapes the content and style of a text.
	CCSS.ELA-Literacy.K-12.R.R.7 Integration of Knowledge and Ideas: Integrate and evaluate content presented in diverse formats and media, including visually and quantitatively, as well as in words.
Activity 2.2: Quilt as High Art	CCSS.ELA-Literacy.11-12.R.I.1 Key Ideas and Details: Cite strong and thorough textual evidence to support analysis of what the text says explicitly as well as inferences drawn from the text, including determining where the text leaves matters uncertain.
	CCSS.ELA-Literacy.11-12.R.I.10 Range of Reading and Level of Text Complexity: By the end of grade 11, read and comprehend literary nonfiction in the grades 11–CCR text complexity band proficiently, with scaffolding as needed at the high end of the range. By the end of grade 12, read and comprehend literary nonfiction at the high end of the grades 11–CCR text complexity band independently and proficiently.

Menu	Common Core State Standards
Activity 2.2: **Quilt as High Art,** *continued*	CCSS.ELA-Literacy.11-12.W.2.b Text Types and Purposes: Develop the topic thoroughly by selecting the most significant and relevant facts, extended definitions, concrete details, quotations, or other information and examples appropriate to the audience's knowledge of the topic.
	CCSS.ELA-Literacy.11-12.SL.1 Comprehension and Collaboration: Initiate and participate effectively in a range of collaborative discussions (one-on-one, in groups, and teacher-led) with diverse partners on grades 11–12 topics, texts, and issues, building on others' ideas and expressing their own clearly and persuasively.
	CCSS.ELA-Literacy.11-12.L.4 Vocabulary Acquisition and Use: Determine or clarify the meaning of unknown and multiple-meaning words and phrases based on grades 11–12 reading and content, choosing flexibly from a range of strategies.
Activity 2.3: **Movie Trailer**	CCSS.ELA-Literacy.K-12.SL.1 Comprehension and Collaboration: Prepare for and participate effectively in a range of conversations and collaborations with diverse partners, building on others' ideas and expressing their own clearly and persuasively.
	CCSS.ELA-Literacy.K-12.SL.2 Comprehension and Collaboration: Integrate and evaluate information presented in diverse media and formats, including visually, quantitatively, and orally.
	CCSS.ELA-Literacy.K-12.SL.3 Comprehension and Collaboration: Evaluate a speaker's point of view, reasoning, and use of evidence and rhetoric.
	CCSS.ELA-Literacy.K-12.W.R.5 Production and Distribution of Writing: Develop and strengthen writing as needed by planning, revising, editing, rewriting, or trying a new approach.
	CCSS.ELA-Literacy.K-12.W.R.6 Production and Distribution of Writing: Use technology, including the Internet, to produce and publish writing and to interact and collaborate with others.
Activity 2.4: **Allegory**	CCSS.ELA-Literacy.11-12.R.L.1 Key Ideas and Details: Cite strong and thorough textual evidence to support analysis of what the text says explicitly as well as inferences drawn from the text, including determining where the text leaves matters uncertain.
	CCSS.ELA-Literacy.11-12.R.L.2 Key Ideas and Details: Determine two or more themes or central ideas of a text and analyze their development over the course of the text, including how they interact and build on one another to produce a complex account; provide an objective summary of the text.
	CCSS.ELA-Literacy.11-12.R.L.10 Range of Reading and Level of Text Complexity: By the end of grade 11, read and comprehend literature, including stories, dramas, and poems, in the grades 11–CCR text complexity band proficiently, with scaffolding as needed at the high end of the range. By the end of grade 12, read and comprehend literature, including stories, dramas, and poems, at the high end of the grades 11–CCR text complexity band independently and proficiently.

Menu	Common Core State Standards
Activity 2.4: Allegory, *continued*	CCSS.ELA-Literacy.11-12.SL.1 Comprehension and Collaboration: Initiate and participate effectively in a range of collaborative discussions (one-on-one, in groups, and teacher-led) with diverse partners on grades 11–12 topics, texts, and issues, building on others' ideas and expressing their own clearly and persuasively.
Chapter 3: Deconstruction	
Activity 3.1: The Soundtrack	CCSS.ELA-Literacy.9-10.R.L.1 Key Ideas and Details: Cite strong and thorough textual evidence to support analysis of what the text says explicitly as well as inferences drawn from the text.
	CCSS.ELA-Literacy.9-10.R.L.10 Range of Reading and Level of Text Complexity: By the end of grade 9, read and comprehend literature, including stories, dramas, and poems, in the grades 9–10 text complexity band proficiently, with scaffolding as needed at the high end of the range. By the end of grade 10, read and comprehend literature, including stories, dramas, and poems, at the high end of the grades 9–10 text complexity band independently and proficiently.
	CCSS.ELA-Literacy.9-10.W.4 Production and Distribution of Writing: Produce clear and coherent writing in which the development, organization, and style are appropriate to task, purpose, and audience. (Grade-specific expectations for writing types are defined in standards 1–3 above.)
	CCSS.ELA-Literacy.9-10.SL.1 Comprehension and Collaboration: Initiate and participate effectively in a range of collaborative discussions (one-on-one, in groups, and teacher-led) with diverse partners on grades 9–10 topics, texts, and issues, building on others' ideas and expressing their own clearly and persuasively.
	CCSS.ELA-Literacy.9-10.SL.5 Presentation of Knowledge and Ideas: Make strategic use of digital media (e.g., textual, graphical, audio, visual, and interactive elements) in presentations to enhance understanding of findings, reasoning, and evidence and to add interest.
Activity 3.2: The Art of Reduction	CCSS.ELA-Literacy.CCRA.R.1 Read closely to determine what the text says explicitly and to make logical inferences from it; cite specific textual evidence when writing or speaking to support conclusions drawn from the text.
	CCSS.ELA-Literacy.CCRA.R.2 Determine central ideas or themes of a text and analyze their development; summarize the key supporting details and ideas.
	CCSS.ELA-Literacy.CCRA.R.3 Analyze how and why individuals, events, or ideas develop and interact over the course of a text.